BY HOOK OR ᴅʏ ᴄ

OUR LANGUAGE HAS EVOLVED

COMPILED BY

TONY WOOTTON AND GWEN ZANZOTTERA

ILLUSTRATIONS BY

Drawing the Line

© Anthony Wootton and Gwenette Zanzottera

ISBN 09539386-0-3

Illustrations by Drawing the Line
Printed by Vale Print & Design (Willersey)

Published by Wootton-Zanzottera

G Zanzottera
18 Childs Close
STRATFORD UPON AVON CV37 0TG
Tel/Fax: 01789 299486
Tel/Fax: 01726 813476   Email: gwenettezan@aol.com

FOREWORD

Tony Wootton and Gwen Zanzottera are Heart of England qualified Blue Badge Guides who have worked for many years touring Stratford upon Avon, Oxford, Birmingham and various parts of the Cotswolds.

They have realised that no visitor wants a stream of dates or bald facts and they have each built up a repertoire of sayings and their origins. Many times they have been asked for a book of these sayings and so decided to put into print the stories and explanations which they use.

Working in Stratford upon Avon (and as Tony was at one time Deputy Chief Guide at Shakespeare's Birthplace) the emphasis in Stratford is naturally upon William Shakespeare and his works. Here was an amazing man who over the years made up hundreds of words which have since passed into the English language, and every day we use quotations of his (sometimes slightly altered from the original) without realising who wrote them, so Gwen and Tony have sprinkled a few of these widely used quotations among the pages.

Since the first edition of this book, Tony has left Stratford for 'fresh fields and pastures new' and is now working at the Eden Project in Cornwall.

ABOVE BOARD

In the Middle Ages, the word 'table' had not yet arrived from France and you ate from a 'board' (a Scandinavian word), supported on trestles.   This board was rough on one side, the side you ate your meals on, and smooth and polished on the other.   The meal was eaten and then the board was turned so that all the scraps fell onto the floor and the polished side was then uppermost (you **took the rough with the smooth**).

The board was used for games, which were marked on the surface of the board, and were thus **board games**.   If you won by a large margin or won all the games you would **sweep the board**, but you had to keep your hands showing to prove that you were not cheating and so everything was **above board**.

The head of the household was the only one of the family to sit in a chair with arms as he was the only person in the house to have idle hands, and so he was the **Chairman** in the house.   If he held a meeting of his servants or estate workers, they all sat round the board and it was a **board meeting** and he was the **Chairman of the Board**.

That which we call a rose by any other name would smell as sweet

> *Romeo and Juliet*

If a band of strolling players came to the village, the farm carts were gathered together and the boards from various homes placed on top of the carts to form a flat surface, and so the actors **trod the boards.**

If visitors came to stay the night and the best bed (reserved for visitors) was full, then the board could be placed on the straw on the floor or left on the supporting trestles to offer **bed and board.**   There was often a ledge round the walls of the room upon which to lodge your bottom while you ate, so if you stayed overnight and then ate with the family, you were offered **board and lodging**.

BACK TO SQUARE ONE

This is a saying which dates back to the nineteen thirties when football matches were broadcast and a plan of the pitch was published, all marked out into squares.   After each move on the pitch, the commentator gave the number of the square so that the listener knew exactly where the action was.   Square one was the goalkeeper's square so when the ball was passed back to the goalkeeper, it was **back to square one**.

All the world's a stage and all the men and women merely players

As You Like It

BEYOND THE PALE

This phrase probably has come from the days of motte and bailey castles In Norman times.   The two ditches round the mound (the motte) were fenced in with a wooden paling fence. Any people misbehaving were put beyond the paling fence, i.e. outside the bounds of the castle and thus outside any protection.

This may be where another saying comes from.   There were often prisoners kept in the wooden tower on the top of the mound and if these prisoners behaved themselves they were sometimes allowed out on the bailey (the area between the two circular ditches) - thus being **let out on bail**.

BLESS YOU

It was thought at one time that when you sneezed your soul jumped out of your body, and so people said **Bless you** to ensure that your soul was not ensnared by the devil and that it jumped safely back into your body.

Double, double, toil and trouble
Macbeth

BONFIRE

Nowadays one has to wait until the last surviving relative of someone buried in a churchyard has died before one can relocate gravestones or disturb any grave, but in the Middle Ages it was the practice to dig up the bones after about 25 or 30 years and put them into the charnel house

When the charnel house became full, the bones were taken out and burned on a **bonefire**, which later became **bonfire**.

BOX OFFICE

In the early days of theatres, such as the Globe theatre in Shakespeare's day, there were no printed tickets and those wishing to attend put a small coin in a sealed box as they went in.   After the performance, this box was taken to small office at the back of the theatre, and the seal broken and the contents counted.

Why then, the world's mine oyster
                    The Merry Wives of Windsor

BOXING DAY

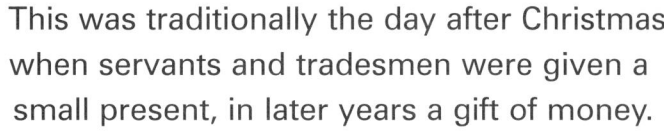

This was traditionally the day after Christmas when servants and tradesmen were given a small present, in later years a gift of money.

This probably dates back to when the leftovers from the Christmas feast of the lord of the manor were divided up and sent round to the estate workers or the poor in a box.

The errand boys in Victorian times used to go round on Boxing Day with a box marked To Insure Prompt Service - which is where our modern word **TIPS** comes from. (Nowadays we use the word 'ensure' rather than 'insure').

BURNING THE CANDLE AT BOTH ENDS

This dates back to when one form of artificial light was a rather primitive candle made from a length of reed dipped in animal fat. This was fitted into a holder which held it round the middle, and then lighted at one end.   Because the resulting light was rather dim, the candle could be bent in half and **burned at both ends** to give a brighter light.   This also gives us our modern variation of a brighter (perhaps more hectic) life, but a shorter one.

Put out the light and then put out the light
Othello

BUYING A PIG IN A POKE

Suckling pigs used to be taken to market in a sack, or poke.   It was advisable not to buy the pig without first opening the poke and checking that there was actually a pig, which was worth money, and not a cat as a substitute. If you did not check, you would be **buying a pig in a poke**.

This could also have given us the saying **to let the cat out of the bag**.

BY HOOK OR BY CROOK

In the Middle Ages, the peasants were only allowed to take from the forests wood which they could reach **by hook or by crook**. The 'hook' was the billhook, or curved sickle and was useful in cutting the brushwood: the crook was the long stick with the curved end - like a shepherd's crook - and with this they could pull down the lower branches of the trees to cut them off.

Rough winds do shake the darling buds of May

Sonnet 18

CARNIVAL

Although now taken to mean any public celebration, and particularly a street procession, it originally came from the Latin phrase meaning 'farewell meat' and was a time of revelry at the beginning of Lent.   In many Catholic countries, this is still the case.

CASH ON THE NAIL

In medieval markets, the nail was a short post by a market stall. As in most markets, goods had to be paid for immediately and the purchaser put his money on the nail: any change was also **paid on the nail**.

COLD SHOULDER

In the Middle Ages, when visitors came to the house it was the custom to offer them food and also, as they had often come long distances, to ask them to stay.   Sometimes, as nowadays, these guests outstayed their welcome.   No-one could be rude and ask them to go, but the solution was simple.   At the main meal of the day, the family was served hot mutton (cooked sheep) and the guests were served cold mutton, usually the rather fatty part of the shoulder.   Thus the guests knew it was time to leave because they had been given **the cold shoulder**.

Neither a borrower nor a lender be
Hamlet

COME UP TO SCRATCH

In the nineteenth century, prizefighting was a very popular sport - though without most of the rules which are well known today. There were no 'rounds' as we know them and the fighting went on until one of the contestants was knocked down. If he failed to recover enough to reach a mark which was scratched across the ground, he was the loser, as he had not **come up to scratch**.

CURFEW

This comes from the Norman French 'couvre feu' meaning to cover the fire or cover the light and dates back to 1066 and the time of the Norman invasion. To stop people meeting and plotting against the invaders, a bell was rung at night and everyone had to be back in their own home, with the shutters up and the light not seen from the outside. In the morning the curfew bell was rung again and everyone could go out and go to work.

O Romeo, Romeo, wherefore art thou Romeo
Romeo and Juliet

DAYLIGHT ROBBERY

This goes back to 1696 when a tax on windows was introduced. This was increased in 1782 when a graduated tax of one old shilling per window was charged up to ten windows, increasing very sharply after that. Rather than pay this tax, which was seen as **daylight robbery**, people bricked up some of their windows and this can often be seen in buildings to this day.

A DUNCE

The original 'dunsers' were followers of a man called Duns Scotus who died in 1308. He is said to have opposed classical studies on the revival of learning and so any opposer to learning was called a **dunce** and it gradually came to mean a blockhead or someone who could not learn.

EATING HUMBLE PIE

This phrase, often used to mean that a person is apologising or backing down in some way, originally meant that someone was humiliated or 'put down'. It came from the practice of the lord of the manor eating the best meat after a day's hunting, particularly stag hunting. The servants and lower orders of the household ate 'umble pie' made out of the liver, heart and entrails of the deer.

EAVESDROPPING

Where a roof comes down to meet the
wall of the house, there is an overhang
to ensure that any water runs off the
roof.   These are the eaves of the
house, and there is sometimes a slight
gap between the roof and the wall to
get rid of any smoke from the fire.

Anyone standing under the eaves of the house can sometimes
hear what is being said within the house - they are
eavesdropping.

FLASH IN THE PAN

This is often used to describe something which is the cause of
sudden excitement or something which has a big show at the
beginning without amounting to anything.

This comes from the days of the old, and
unreliable, flintlock gun and meant that
there was a flash in the lock pan
of the gun, without the gun
actually firing or being effective.

Though this be madness, yet there is method.
Hamlet

FREELANCE

This dates back to the Crusades and the
many knights and men-at-arms who
wandered around Europe hoping to be hired
as mercenaries.   Their lances were not being used in
any battle at that particular moment, and so were free, i.e.
could be hired by the highest bidder.

HAVETH LANCE
WILT TRAVEL

FREEZE THE BALLS OFF A BRASS MONKEY

On the old sailing ships, the iron cannonballs were often piled
up like tins in a supermarket onto a wooden triangle.   On the
Admiral's ship they were piled on a brass triangle or sometimes
a brass tray.

If it were very cold, the brass would naturally get smaller and
the cannonballs (not contracting at the same rate as the brass)
would fall off and roll all over the deck.   The triangle was known
as a monkey, so the sailors
used to say that **it was cold
enough to freeze the balls off
a brass monkey**.

For sale: one set of genuine
Siberian Brass Monkeys
[slightly incomplete]

A pair of star-crossed lovers
                    Romeo and Juliet

A FROG IN THE THROAT

In medieval times one of the old folk cures for a sore throat or a cough was to dangle a little yellow frog headfirst into the throat. The frog would give out some stringy saliva which the patient had to swallow slowly.   The frog would often struggle and its feet might aggravate the soreness, so making the patient hoarse and so he **had a frog in his throat**.

Amazingly, in the twentieth century it was discovered that there was an efficient antibiotic in frog saliva!

I didn't say swallow the WHOLE FROG

GETTING THE SACK

Many years ago when a man would save up and buy the tools of his trade, he would carry them round in a sack.   When he got a job he handed over his sack of tools for the employer to look after, so when he was dismissed he was given back his sack.

If music be the food of love, play on
Twelfth Night

GO ON STRIKE

Although more usually associated with modern day factories, this saying actually dates from the eighteenth century and sailors.   Life at sea was very hard and sometimes the sailors would rebel by striking, or lowering, the sails of the ship and refusing to raise them, so that the ship could sail, until someone listened to them and tried to improve their conditions.

I agree I said "strike the mainsail"   I didn't say anything about throwing it over the side . .

HUNG FOR A SHEEP AS A LAMB

In medieval times sheep stealing was punishable by hanging. It was pointless, therefore, just to steal a lamb which would not go very far in feeding the family.   If you were going to be hung anyway, a sheep would go much further in fending off starvation, and so **you** might **as well be hung for a sheep as a lamb**.

This was the most unkindest cut of all.
Julius Caesar

IN THE NICK OF TIME

This refers to the way in which scores were kept in various games, where a man would cut a notch or a 'nick' in the side of a stick (known as a tally stick) whenever a team scored.

Where a side scored in the last moments of the game, it was known as a 'nick in time' and this has now become **in the nick of time**.

OUR FINEST SEASON

LEFT ON THE SHELF

When families had a lot of daughters, it was necessary to keep them safe from visitors and perhaps even the servants, so a sleep loft was built - a ledge about halfway up the wall and reached by a ladder.

The straw mattresses of the daughters of the house were placed in a row on this ledge and there they slept until they married. The unmarried girls were, of course, **left on the shelf**.

To sleep, perchance to dream.
Hamlet

LOCK, STOCK AND BARREL

The barrel in this saying has nothing to do with drink, but the saying goes back to guns. The stock of a gun is a piece you put to your shoulder, the lock is where the initial firing takes place and the barrel where the shot comes out, so the whole gun is composed of **lock, stock and barrel** and the phrase is used to mean absolutely everything, for instance 'the shop was cleared out lock, stock and barrel'.

LOOSE WOMAN

In Shakespeare's day a girl wore her hair loose until she reached maidenhood and then she put up her hair - pinned it up tidily onto the top of her head. The only time she **let her hair down** was when she walked to Church on her wedding day. If she wore her hair down at any other time, she was a **loose woman**.

Incidentally, the only other women who had their hair flowing were those who were mad, and so Ophelia is shown in paintings floating in the water with her hair streaming out.

It is a wise man that knows his own son
Merchant of Venice

LUNATIC

This comes from the Latin 'luna' meaning a moon and can mean someone who goes mad with the changes of the moon.

However, it is more usually associated with the old belief that if the moon shone on you while you were asleep, it sent you mad - you became a **lunatic**. This is one reason why the old thatched roofs came so far down over the windows, to prevent the moon shining on someone asleep.

MAD AS A HATTER

This is not from the book 'Alice in Wonderland', but dates back before that when many people wore top hats.   Because the hatter worked very close to the hat while he was making it and brushing it smooth, one of the chemicals used in hat making was breathed in over a long period of time and gradually sent the hatter insane.

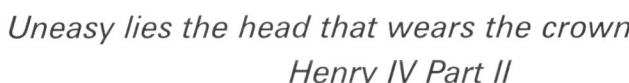

Uneasy lies the head that wears the crown
Henry IV Part II

A MOP FAIR

In many places the annual fair is known as 'The Mop', and this is a shortened form of 'Mop Fair'.   Anyone looking for work would at one time line up at The Mop and they would carry the tools of their trade, i.e. a milking stool, a bag of carpenter's tools, or a mop.   They would be inspected by the employers who walked along the line, and then offered a job.

In some places, there would be a Runaway Mop about two weeks later and this was for anyone hired at the Mop who did not like their employer.   They could run away and line up at the Runaway Mop to see if they could find a better job.

NOT ENOUGH ROOM TO SWING A CAT

This, as in the case of so many other sayings, goes back to the days of sailing ships and refers to the 'cat o' nine tails', or whip with nine thongs used on sailors.   As the cabins and crews' quarters below decks were very small, there was **not enough room to swing a cat** and so the sailors were whipped up on deck.

O brave new world
> *The Tempest*

ON THE CADGE

This saying is used nowadays to describe someone who is scrounging or trying to get something for nothing. It goes back to medieval times when the Lord of the Manor used birds of prey for hunting.

The frame on which a falcon was carried was a 'cadge' and any of the tenants or peasants who were given the job of carrying the cadge all day, were thought to be doing very little for their day's wages.

ON TENTERHOOKS

A 'tenter' is a frame for stretching cloth (which is where the word 'tent' comes from), and the 'tenterhook' is the hook which holds the cloth taut, particularly after treating and washing.

This is why when someone's nerves are stretched to the utmost and they are tense and taut, they are described as being **on tenterhooks**.

My salad days
> *Antony and Cleopatra*

POP GOES THE WEASEL

In the last century there was a children's song which went 'Up and down the City Road, in and out the Eagle, that's the way the money goes, pop goes the weasel'. It had nothing to do with animals, particularly as it was set in London.

A weasel was the tool which hatters used and as many of them worked near the City Road, when they needed money (especially for drink at the Eagle pub in the City Road), they would 'pop' or pawn the weasel in the nearest pawnbrokers.

POT LUCK

In the Middle Ages, although many large pieces of meat were roasted on a spit, there was always a large pot hanging

"More gravy anyone?"

over the fire. The contents of this pot could have been bubbling away for three days or three weeks and all the odds and ends went into this pot, such as bones which had been gnawed free of meat, odd scraps of meat, sundry vegetables, and even anything which fell down the chimney! Visitors would be handed a square piece of bread to act as a plate and told to take **pot luck**.

Murder most foul
> *Hamlet*

RED HERRING

Although more commonly used today in popular murder mysteries, the saying does in fact go back to fox hunting.

A red herring was a bloater (a herring partially dried in smoke) and this was often dragged across the

"At least he smells better than a partially dried herring"

trail of a fox to confuse the pursuing hounds. They would follow the false trail - the **red herring**.

ROBBING PETER TO PAY PAUL

This is a saying which goes back to the sixteenth century. St Peter's in Westminster, which had only just been created a cathedral, was put back to being just an abbey Church.   The estates belonging to the Church, and their income, were used to pay for urgent repairs to St Paul's cathedral, so the Church authorities **robbed Peter to pay Paul**.

Ill met by moonlight
A Midsummer Night's Dream

SALARY

This comes from Roman times when salt was essential and soldiers were either paid part of their wages in salt or were given 'salt money' or salarium.

This also gives us another saying, because when someone has not earned their keep, we say they are **not worth their salt**.

SCOT FREE

A 'scot' was a payment, particularly of a tax, so to **get off scot free** meant that you did not have to pay the customary tax on something.

SENT TO COVENTRY

This dates back to the seventeenth century and the English Civil War. Coventry supported the Parliamentarians (under Oliver Cromwell) and any Royalist prisoners (who supported Charles I) who were **sent to Coventry** were not befriended by anyone at all. In fact, if they were let out into the city occasionally, the citizens of Coventry refused to speak to them.

Lord what fools these mortals be
A Midsummer Night's Dream

SHIP-SHAPE AND BRISTOL FASHION

This goes back to the fifteenth century when Bristol was one of the most important ports in England.   Any sea voyage was highly dangerous and all ships and their equipment had to be in the best possible condition.   Bristol enjoyed the reputation that the workers there did everything to ensure the safety of the voyagers and so anything which was neat, tidy and carefully set out was known as being **ship-shape and Bristol fashion**.

SHOW A LEG

Sometimes the sailors on sailing ships took women on the voyage and they would often take their girlfriends into the hammock for the night.   In the morning the bosun would come round to wake up the sailors and would shout 'show a leg'.

If the leg which hung over the side of the hammock were a nice smooth one, it obviously belonged to a female and they were allowed to stay in bed for a while longer, but a hairy leg belonged to a sailor and he would be immediately expected to jump out and go to work.   (Of course, the sailors soon got wise to this and started to shave their legs.)

All that glisters is not gold (usually quoted as 'glitters')
Merchant of Venice

SLEEP TIGHT

In Elizabethan times, beds were often made of a wooden frame supported on legs and then rope was woven from side to side and top to bottom of the frame. This rope supported the mattress and bedclothes, but sleeping for a time on this rope made it go slack and this was uncomfortable. There was a wooden tool provided to pull the rope taut and this was much more comfortable, in other words it was far better to **sleep tight**, which is why we now say 'Goodnight, sleep tight'.

SOAP OPERA

This dates back to the nineteen thirties and forties when the idea of having daily serials on the radio started in America. Each day the story ended with melodramatic suspense and listeners had to wait until the  next day to see the outcome of that particular part of the plot.

In America, radio was sponsored by advertising and it was the soap companies who sponsored these daily serials, which became known as **soap operas**.

Friends, Romans and countrymen lend me your ears
Julius Caesar

SPOONING

In Elizabethan times, when a young man went to 'court' a girl, he would have to sit with her in the family home, 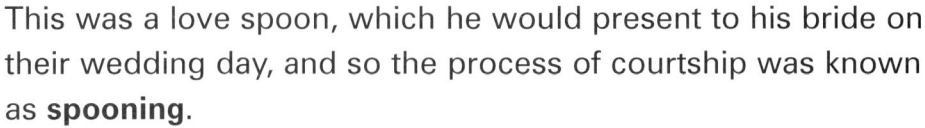 usually under the watchful eye of her father.   The young man would be given a piece of wood which he would have to carve into a spoon, with intricate and romantic patterns on.

This was a love spoon, which he would present to his bride on their wedding day, and so the process of courtship was known as **spooning**.

STOP GAP

The opening on a bread oven was known as the 'gap' and the separate door - which was only used while the bread was cooking - was known as a 'stop' or 'stop-gap'.

From this, a **stop gap** has come to mean anything which is a temporary closure, or a temporary measure.

I cannot tell what the dickens his name is
The Merry Wives of Windsor

SWINGING THE LEAD

In the early days of navigation, it was essential to find the depth of the water, particularly nearer to the land, and the way to do this was to drop a rope over the side of the ship.   The rope was knotted at fathom intervals and there was a lead weight at the bottom of the rope to ensure that it went to the bottom, and didn't just go with the current of the water.

A lazy sailor wouldn't just throw the rope over the side, but would waste time by **swinging the lead** backwards and forwards several times.

TEETOTAL

This is a word which describes someone who does not drink, in other words who practices total abstinence from alcohol.

In the mid nineteenth century, Richard Turner of Preston was a great believer in total abstinence and a member of the Temperance Society.   However, he had a bad stutter and when asked what he advocated, he said t-t-total abstinence and as people made fun of him, the word **teetotal** evolved.

Goodnight, goodnight, parting is such sweet sorrow
Romeo and Juliet

TELL IT TO THE MARINES

A lot of people think that this was first said in the Second World War, but in fact it goes back long before that.

Sailors used to think that the marines were not worth anything at all and would believe anything told to them, and Sir Walter Scott first coined the phrase when he wrote '**tell that to the marines**, the sailors won't believe it'.

THE LOO

"...gardez l'eau!!!"

This is used quite commonly for a lavatory and is said to come from the phrase 'gardez l'eau' (be careful of the water) to warn unsuspecting people below when chamberpots were emptied out of the window of an upper storey of a house into the street.

THRESHOLD

The floors in houses in medieval times were covered with straw, or threshings. As they became muddy or mouldy, a fresh layer was put on top and this became higher and higher through the year. There was a board across the doorway to hold the threshings in place and this was, rather obviously, the **threshold**.

The lady doth protest too much, methinks
                    Hamlet

THE 'V' SIGN

The English archers were the most accurate in Europe and, after the Battle of Agincourt, their fame was assured.   Whenever the French captured English archers they cut off the first two fingers of the hand which drew the bow so that never again would they be able to use a bow.

However, when the English captured French soldiers the English would walk up and down the lines of captives, holding the first two fingers of their right hand upright to show that they were English archers and they still could draw a bow.

TO BOYCOTT

This has come to mean completely ignoring a person or having nothing to do with a person or a company's goods.

It comes from Captain Boycott, a very strict and unbending landlord in Ireland, who refused to allow starving tenants time to pay arrears of rent and had them evicted.   His servants and others refused to work for him and tradespeople would not deal with him, and so he was **boycotted**.

Once more unto the breach, dear friends, once more
Henry V

TO PUT A SPOKE IN YOUR WHEEL

This comes from the days when cartwheels were solid except for one or two holes into which a long round wooden pin could be placed.   This would act as a brake to stop the wheel turning or the cart running away and now if you want to stop someone doing something or carrying out a plan, you **put a spoke in their wheel**.

TO STRIKE WHILE THE IRON IS HOT

This goes back to the days of the blacksmith and refers to the fact that he would know when the iron for the horseshoe was exactly the right temperature to be hammered and bent into the correct shape and size.

Nowadays, when seizing an opportunity or acting at precisely the right time, we are said to **strike while the iron is hot**.

A horse, a horse, my kingdom for a horse
Richard III

UNDER THE THUMB

In medieval times, the fire in the
kitchen of the house was very
important and it was never allowed to go
out, being banked up at night to ensure that it
could just be poked into life in the morning.
Lighting it was a complicated job, particularly
as there were no matches at that time and one
had to use a flint and tinder to strike a spark.

If the housewife was so stupid as to let the fire go out, her
husband was entitled to beat her but it must be with a stick no
thicker than his thumb.   She was definitely **under his thumb**.

UPPER CRUST

The bread oven was filled with wood and the fire was lit and this
burned until the bricks were very hot.   The ashes were then
raked out and the dough was put directly onto the bricks to
bake, the oven being sealed by a wooden door.   Some of the
ashes would stick to the bottom of the loaf and this dirty part of
the bread was given either to the servants or to the poor, with
the better **upper crust** given to the more important members of
the family.

Is this a dagger which I see before me
Macbeth

32

THE WEAKEST GO TO THE WALL

In the Middle Ages, it was law that everyone had to go to Church on Sunday.   Sometimes the Lord of the Manor had a small private chapel, with seats for the family, but the main body of the Church had no seats and the rest of the villagers stood.

Round the walls inside the Church there were stone ledges built into the wall, and these were for the old and infirm to sit on during the service, so **the weakest would go to the wall**.

WELSH RABBIT

In the nineteen twenties and thirties this was a very popular dish of melted cheese (sometimes mixed with ale) on toast, and occasionally referred to on menus as 'Welsh rarebit'.

In fact, it goes back much further to the sixteenth century when only the rich people in Wales could afford the game from the royal game preserves in Wales, and so poor people had never tasted rabbit.   Cheese on toast they could afford, and so they referred to it, jokingly, as their **Welsh rabbit**.

To be or not to be, that is the question
                    Hamlet

A WHIPPING BOY

This phrase is often used when an innocent person is blamed and punished for something which someone else has done.

It dates back to the Middle Ages when it was unthinkable to punish a royal prince by any means, but especially by whipping. A commoner boy, of similar age to the prince (and who had often been educated alongside him) was whipped whenever the royal prince did anything really wrong.

A WHITE ELEPHANT

A white elephant is usually taken to mean something given to a person and which is completely useless, and often very expensive.

"As you can see ladies & gentleman a wide elephant"

At one time, in Eastern countries, a white elephant was sacred and could not be harmed or killed. If there were someone whom you disliked, you gave them a white elephant in the certain knowledge that they would have to look after it and the feeding of it would certainly ruin them.

Blow, blow thou winter wind
As you like it

Alls Well That Ends Well